Elephant Rocks

Elephant Rocks

Kay Ryan

Grove Press
New York

Grateful acknowledgment is made to the following publications, in which these poems first appeared: *Alaska Quarterly Review:* "Apogee," "Distance," "The Woman Who Wrote Too Much." *The Georgia Review:* "Connections," "Full Measure," "Losses." *The New Yorker:* "A Cat/A Future," "A Plain Ordinary Steel Needle Can Float on Pure Water," "Crustacean Island," "Hope," "If She Only Had One Minute," "Mirage Oases," "Relief," "Surfaces" "Swept Up Whole," "That Vase of Lilacs," "Why Isn't It All More Marked." *The Paris Review:* "Bestiary," "Crib," "Poetry in Translation." *Partisan Review:* "Outsider Art," "Doubt." *South Coast Poetry Journal:* "To the Young Anglerfish." *The Southern Review:* "Living with Stripes."

"Outsider Art" also appeared in *The Best American Poetry 1995* (Simon & Schuster, 1995).

Printed in the United States of America
Published simultaneously in Canada

Library of Congress Cataloging-in-Publication Data

Ryan, Kay.
    Elephant rocks: poems / by Kay Ryan.
      p. cm.
    ISBN-10: 0-8021-3525-0 (pbk.)
    ISBN-13: 978-0-8021-3525-4
    I. Title.
    PS3568.Y38E43 1996   811'.54—dc20   95-42668

DESIGN BY LAURA HAMMOND HOUGH

Grove Press
an imprint of Grove/Atlantic, Inc.
841 Broadway
New York, NY 10003

Distributed by Publishers Group West

www.groveatlantic.com

10 11 12   10 9 8 7 6 5

for Carol

For their presence at critical passes, the author wishes to thank Jane Hirshfield, George Bradley, and the Ingram Merrill Foundation.

Contents

Living with Stripes

In tigers, zebras,
and other striped creatures,
any casual posture
plays one beautiful set of lines
against another:
herringbones and arrows
appear and disappear;
chevrons widen and narrow.
Miniature themes and counterpoints
occur in the flexing and extending
of the smaller joints.
How can they stand to drink,
when lapping further complicates
the way the water duplicates their lines?
Knowing how their heads will zigzag out,
I wonder if they dread to start sometimes.

Doubt

A chick has just so much time
to chip its way out, just so much
egg energy to apply to the weakest spot
or whatever spot it started at.
It can't afford doubt. Who can?
Doubt uses albumen
at twice the rate of work.
One backward look by any of us
can cost what it cost Orpheus.
Neither may you answer
the stranger's knock;
you know it is the Person from Porlock
who eats dreams for dinner,
his napkin stained the most delicate colors.

Mirage Oases

First among places
susceptible to trespass
are mirage oases

whose graduated pools
and shaded grasses, palms
and speckled fishes give
before the lightest pressure
and are wrecked.

For they live
only in the kingdom
of suspended wishes,

thrive only at our pleasure
checked.

Cirque

Even the clean
blue-green water
of the cirque,
with nothing
in between
the snow and it
but slant
can't speed
the work,
must wait
upon whatever
makes it white
to dissipate.
It seems
so hard to think
that even lakes
so pure

should start opaque,
that something
always
has to recombine
or sink.

That Vase of Lilacs

Not just lilacs
are like that;
other purples also
leave us vacant
portals, susceptible
to vagrant spirits.
But take that vase
of lilacs: who goes
near it is erased.
In spite of Proust,
the senses don't
attach us to a place
or time: we're *used*
by sweetness—
taken, defenseless,
invaded by a line
of Saracens,
Picts, Angles,

double rows of
fragrance-loving
ancients—people
matched casually
by nose in an
impersonal and
intermittent immortality
of purple.

Chemistry

Words especially
are subject to
the chemistry
of death: it is
an acid bath
which dissolves
or doubles
their strength.
Sentiments
which pleased
drift down
as sediment;
iron trees
grow from filament.

Connections

Connections *lie in wait*—
something that in
the ordinary line of offenses
makes offense more great.
They entrap, they solicit
under false pretenses,
they premeditate.
They tie one of
your shoelaces
to one of a stranger,
they tie strings to purses
and snatch as
you lean down, eager
for a little something *gratis.*

Dew

As neatly as peas
in their green canoe,
as discretely as beads
strung in a row,
sit drops of dew
along a blade of grass.
But unattached and
subject to their weight,
they slip if they accumulate.
Down the green tongue
out of the morning sun
into the general damp,
they're gone.

Lacquer Artist

There is a nacreous gleam
in certain areas of the mind
where something must have been
at some time—
perhaps many somethings,
judging by the pearlescence;
maybe the same weightless pleasures
or the same elusive lessons
repeated and repeated
with the patience
of the lacquer artist seated
at his task—eighty
coats per Japanese box.

All Shall Be Restored

The grains shall be collected
from the thousand shores
to which they found their way,
and the boulder restored,
and the boulder itself replaced
in the cliff, and likewise
the cliff shall rise
or subside until the plate of earth
is without fissure. Restoration
knows no half-measure. It will
not stop when the treasured and lost
bronze horse remounts the steps.
Even this horse will founder backward
to coin, cannon, and domestic pots,
which themselves shall bubble and
drain back to green veins in stone.

And every word written shall lift off
letter by letter, the backward text
read ever briefer, ever more antic
in its effort to insist that nothing
shall be lost.

Full Measure

You will get your full measure.
But, as when asking fairies for favors,
there is a trick: it comes in a block.
And of course one block is not
like another. Some respond to water,
giving everything wet a little flavor.
Some succumb to heat like butter.
Others give to steady pressure.
Others shatter at a tap. But
some resist; nothing in nature softens up
their bulk and no personal attack works.
People whose gift will not break
live by it all their lives; it shadows
every empty act they undertake.

Stars of Bethlehems

Throughout the sky
there are cinders
black as the night.
These are unborn stars
awaiting their source of light.

The night is gritty
with things to hit,
should something
go on in a city
or the outskirts of it.

Crib

From the Greek for
woven or *plaited,*
which quickly translated
to *basket.* Whence the verb
crib, which meant "to filch"
under cover of wicker
anything—some liquor,
a cutlet.
For we want to make off
with things that are not
our own. There is a pleasure
theft brings, a vitality
to the home.
Cribbed objects or answers
keep their guilty shimmer
forever, have you noticed?
Yet religions downplay this.

Note, for instance, in our
annual rehearsals of innocence,
the substitution of *manger* for *crib*—
as if we ever deserved that baby,
or thought we did.

Bestiary

A bestiary catalogs
bests. The mediocres
both higher and lower
are suppressed in favor
of the singularly savage
or clever, the spectacularly
pincered, the archest
of the arch deceivers
who press their advantage
without quarter even after
they've won as of course they would.
Best is not to be confused with *good*—
a different creature altogether,
and treated of in the goodiary—
a text alas lost now for centuries.

How Birds Sing

One is not taxed;
one need not practice;
one simply tips
the throat back
over the spine axis
and asserts the chest.
The wings and the rest
compress a musical
squeeze which floats
a series of notes
upon the breeze.

How a Thought Thinks

A thought is dumb,
without eyes, ears,
opposable thumb,
or a tongue.
A thought lives
underground, not
wholly moleish
but with some
of the same
disinterests.
The amazing thing
is that it isn't helpless.
Of all creatures
it is the most
random eater.
Caring only for travel
it eats whatever
roots, ants, or gravel
it meets. It occupies

no more space
than moles. We know it
only by some holes
and the way
apparently healthy notions
topple in the garden.

Intention

Intention doesn't sweeten.
It should be picked young
and eaten. Sometimes only hours
separate the cotyledon
from the wooden plant.
Then if you want to eat it,
you can't.

If the Moon Happened Once

If the moon happened *once,*
it wouldn't matter much,
would it?

One evening's ticket
punched with a
round or a crescent.

You could like it
or not like it,
as you chose.

It couldn't alter
every time it rose;

it couldn't do those
things with scarves
it does.

New Clothes

The emperor who
was tricked by the tailors
is familiar to you.

But the tailors
keep on changing
what they do
to make money.

(*Tailor* means
to make something
fit somebody.)

Be guaranteed
that they will discover
your pride.

You will cast aside
something you cherish
when the tailors whisper,
"Only you could wear this."

It is almost never clothes
such as the emperor bought

but it is always something close
to something you've got.

Simply by Growing Larger

Simply by growing larger, any object will suffer continual decrease in relative surface area.

—Stephen Jay Gould

As a thing grows larger,
it grows darker.
The dense organs flourish.
More and more blood goes to nourish
the purplish lobes
and loops of sausage,
all slickly packaged.
Once-agile limbs are now fragile
Humpty-Dumpty legs and arms.
Whatever charms the small thing had
are history. This is
particularly cruel in spring,
when simpler hearts can
flush and blanch a pair of wings
in one exchange, and sense
is one cell deep, and things
aren't sullied. Then it is strange
to be the one who chanced to keep,
to grow gravid and broad-bellied.

To the Young Anglerfish

The angler's lure required 500 separate modifications to attain its exquisite mimicry.

—*Stephen Jay Gould*

For now and for the next 400-plus generations,
the hornlike symptom on your brow
will itch and be subject to irritation.
At that point it will begin to resemble a
    modification
useful for tricking food. It will at last begin
to begin to do some good.
Meanwhile, the problems of life enhance:
an awkwardness attends the mating dance
and an inexplicable thoughtfulness
at the wrong moments.
That part of you that is pledged to the future
abstracts you in some way from nature
with the small *n*. You feel a
comical, budding power, and then
you don't again.

Crustacean Island

There could be an island paradise
where crustaceans prevail.
Click, click, go the lobsters
with their china mitts and
articulated tails.
It would not be sad like whales
with their immense and patient sieving
and the sobering modesty
of their general way of living.
It would be an island blessed
with only cold-blooded residents
and no human angle.
It would echo with a thousand castanets
and no flamencos.

Creatures of the Margins

There are the creatures of the margins
soft and translucent and not at all
unpleasant unless they get too much light
which hardens and darkens the denizens
of margins like raisins. They cannot
continue their work if they stiffen
for there as everywhere work depends
upon motion. So learn not to check
the sedges or fish around the edges
of the known. They turn brown.

Imaginary Eskimos

Who knows
if Eskimos
choose to go
with floes
or just go,
regretting motion,
missing a fixed position
vis-à-vis the ocean.
It is common
to suppose
that anyone
whom one is not
is predisposed
to like her lot—
that when she
drills down
through the ice

to fish
and sees the black
and restless drift
and works against
the cold occlusion
which always threatens,
it is easier
for that sort of person.

Outsider Art

Most of it's too dreary
or too cherry red.
If it's a chair, it's
covered with things
the savior said
or should have said—
dense admonishments
in nail polish
too small to be read.
If it's a picture,
the frame is either
burnt matches glued together
or a regular frame painted over
to extend the picture. There never
seems to be a surface equal
to the needs of these people.
Their purpose wraps
around the backs of things
and under arms;

they gouge and hatch
and glue on charms
till likable materials—
apple crates and canning funnels—
lose their rural ease. We are not
pleased the way we thought
we would be pleased.

Caught

If something
gets caught
like a bone
in the throat
it isn't right.

We know this
with fish:

it isn't impolite
to cough.
Our life
is at risk.

But there are
so many wrong thoughts
we refuse to release

massaging
our own throats
like pâté geese.

Salts

It makes no sense
that we seek what we need
where it is least dense

inviting home beasts
that we can't explain

putting up with the
ox's noxious musk,
hyena hairs in drains,
the effect on chairs
of elephants in chains

for the sake of a
secret flake of skin
or grain or scrape
of wild boar's tusk

furtively decocted
to table salt
available in boxes.

Les Petites Confitures

(The Little Jams)

These three pieces
in Satie's elegant notation
were just discovered
at the Métro station
where he rolled them
in a *Figaro* of April twenty-second,
nineteen twenty-seven,
and put them in a pipe
two inches in diameter, the type
then commonly used for banisters.
They are three sticky pieces
for piano or banjo—
each instrument to be played
so as to sound like the other.
That is really the hub
of the amusement. Each piece
lasts about a minute.

When they were first tried
after being in the pipe,
they kept rolling back up.
Really, keeping them flat
was half the banjo-piano
man's work.

Why Isn't It All More Marked

Why isn't it all
more marked,
why isn't every wall
graffitied, every park tree
stripped like the
stark limbs
in the house of
the chimpanzees?
Why is there bark
left? Why do people
cling to their
shortening shrifts
like rafts? So
silent.
Not why people *are;*
why not *more* violent?
We must be
so absorbent.

We must be
almost crystals,
almost all some
neutralizing chemical
that really does
clarify and bring peace,
take black sorrow
and make surcease.

Witness

Never trust a witness.
By the time a thing is
noticed, it has happened.
Some magician's redirected
our attention to the rabbit.
The best life is suspected,
not examined.
And never trust reverse.
The mourners of the dead
count backward from the date
of the event, rehearsing
its approach, investing
final words with greatest weight,
as though weight ever
carried what we meant;
as though he could have
told us where he went.

Learning

Whatever must be learned
is always on the bottom,
as with the law of drawers
and the necessary item.
It isn't pleasant,
whatever they tell children,
to turn out on the floor
the folded things in them.

Apogee

At high speeds
we know
when an orbit
starts to go
backwards:
on fair rides
like the Hammer
or in airplane disasters,
our brains are
plastered to
one wall of the skull
or another;
we comprehend reverse
through the
sudden compression
of matter.

In a way it's worse
when the turn's wider—
say a boat on a soft tide
in mild water—
we hardly knew
that we were floating out.
The sense of turning back
seems like our fault.

Killing Time

Time is rubbery.
If you hide it
in the shrubbery
it will wait
till winter and
wash back out
with the rainwater.
You will find it
on your steps again
like the newspaper.
Time compresses.
Stuff it in the
couch corner and
it will spring out
some night or other
when you have guests.
One of whom guesses.
Time stretches.

Then it snaps back
leaving bare patches
that didn't happen.
Abandoned time hardens
like hidden gum.
People feel around.
Sooner or later
it will be found.

Against Gravity

How do we move
under weight?
What opposite force
do we generate
that keeps our clothes
floating around us,
for instance, or goes
any distance toward
explaining our fondness
for jumping?
Some pump,
like a fish tank's, maybe;
some auto-aeration or something.
Because we're glad some mornings,
and buoyant, as though we had
no bombs or appointments.

Lacunae

Lacunae aren't
what was going to be
empty anyway.
They aren't spaces
with uses, such as
margins or highway edges.
Lacunae are losses
in the middles of places—
drops where something
documented happened
but the document is
gone—pond shaped
or jagged.

Intransigence

Intransigence is the main fault—or the great virtue—of the Saties.
　　　　　　　—Pierre-Daniel Templier, Eric Satie

Intransigence
as a quality
rejects influence
and encourages oddity.

I will not be moved
it says most movingly
to anyone
touched by irony.

For intransigence
lives in a host
and like all guests
must pay a cost.

It is worn
and worked at by mortality.
The flesh erodes
beneath it gradually.

What was fierce
becomes cantankerous.
It is cruel for the host
and for intransigence.

Age

As some people age
they kinden.
The apertures
of their eyes widen.
I do not think they weaken;
I think something weak strengthens
until they are more and more it,
like letting in heaven.
But other people are
mussels or clams, frightened.
Steam or knife blades mean open.
They hear heaven, they think boiled or broken.

Counsel

It is possible
that even the best counsel
cannot be processed
by the body.
All supplements to
our personal chemistry
are screened by tiny
fanatical secret organs
that refuse much more than
they accept. It is hard
to add even minerals.
Iron tablets, for example,
are not correct
and pass through us like
windowless alien crafts.
What the body wants is so exact.

Insult

Insult is injury
taken personally,
saying, *This is not*
a random fracture
that would have happened
to any leg out there;
this was a conscious unkindness.
We need insult to remind us
that we aren't always just hurt,
that there are some sources—
even in the self, parts of which
tread on other parts with such boldness
that we must say, *You must stop this.*

Silence

Silence is not snow.
It cannot grow
deeper. A thousand years
of it are thinner
than paper. So
we must have it
all wrong
when we feel trapped
like mastodons.

A Cat/A Future

A cat can draw
the blinds
behind her eyes
whenever she
decides. Nothing
alters in the stare
itself but she's
not there. Likewise
a future can occlude:
still sitting there,
doing nothing rude.

Hope

What's the use
of something
as unstable
and diffuse as hope—
the almost-twin
of making-do,
the isotope
of going on:
what isn't in
the envelope
just before
it isn't:
the always tabled
righting of the present.

Losses

Most losses add something—
a new socket or silence,
a gap in a personal
archipelago of islands.

We have that difference
to visit—itself
a going-on of sorts.

But there are other losses
so far beyond report
that they leave holes
in holes only

like the ends of the
long and lonely lives
of castaways
thought dead but not.

The Cabinet of Curiosities

It's hard for
minor monsters
born with more
of one thing
than others—
the curse of
double vision
in a single head,
or double ears.
If they are people
their careers
are always troubled—
self-accused,
God-hobbled—
the spilling cup
they took for a blessing—
their lives spent
mopping up,
apologizing.

To Explain the Solitary

It's easy to think a moor or heath
or penury or a limp or a strain
of madness in the family could explain
the solitary, but there are daily
reports of people overriding
the most exotic restraints
to become ordinary. The armless woman
uses her toes to woodburn kittens.
The blind man demonstrates vacuums
and sells lots of them, as convinced
of lint as the next person. Shall I go on?
At the extremities, the furthest Galápago
or worst prison teases all the ordinary
    occupations
from a few birds blown wrong. There is no place
where most people don't adjust. Amherst
didn't curse Miss Dickinson
or Ireland hurt Yeats into song.

Her Politeness

It's her politeness
one loathes: how she
isn't insistent, how
she won't impose, how
nothing's so urgent
it won't wait. Like
a meek guest you tolerate
she goes her way—the muse
you'd have leap at your throat,
you'd spring to obey.

Bad Patch

It is not comical like grease
with its brief release from traction
where a Model T spins off
and liberates a crate of chickens
to the cooking pots of poor Italians.
It was not witnessed.
There was no vehicle.
It is too late
to call for sets,
hire on people.

Swept Up Whole

You aren't *swept up whole,*
however it feels. You're
atomized. The wind passes.
You recongeal. It's
a surprise.

Any Morning

Any morning
can turn molten
without warning.
Every object
can grow fluent.
Suddenly the kitchen
has a sulfur river
through it;
there is a burping
from the closet,
a release of
caustic gases
from the
orange juice glasses.
The large appliances
are bonding in a way

that isn't pleasant
on linoleum as friable
as bacon. We never
fathom how we caused it,
or why we
never see it coming
like Hawaii.

Relief

We know it is close
to something lofty.
Simply getting over being sick
or finding lost property
has in it the leap,
the purge, the quick humility
of witnessing a birth—
how love seeps up
and retakes the earth.
There is a dreamy
wading feeling to your walk
inside the current
of restored riches,
clocks set back,
disasters averted.

Part Midas

The trick would be to be
part Midas—to have
a switch inside us
we could flick at our
pleasure. It would be
nice to plate a chalice
or turn the neighbor's dog
to treasure or add
mettle to lettuce—
to practice playful
acts of malice, table-
top amusements—
stopping short
of where the goblets
started breeding goblets.

The Woman Who Wrote Too Much

I have written
over the doors
of the various
houses and stores
where friends
and supplies were.

Now I can't
locate them anymore
and must shout
general appeals
in the street.

It is a miracle
to me now—
when a piece
of the structure unseals

and there is a dear one,
coming out,
with something
for me to eat.

Surfaces

Surfaces serve
their own purposes,
strive to remain
constant (all lives
want that). There is
a skin, not just on
peaches but on oceans
(note the telltale
slough of foam on beaches).
Sometimes it's loose,
as in the case
of cats: you feel how a
second life slides
under it. Sometimes it
fits. Take glass.
Sometimes it outlasts
its underside. Take reefs.

The private lives of surfaces
are innocent, not devious.
Take the one-dimensional
belief of enamel in itself,
the furious autonomy
of luster (crush a pearl—
it's powder), the whole
curious seamlessness
of how we're each surrounded
and what it doesn't teach.

Sonnet to Spring

The brown, unpleasant,
aggressively ribbed and
unpliant leaves of the loquat,
shaped like bark canoes that
something squashed flat,
litter the spring cement.
A fat-cheeked whim of air—
a French *vent* or some similar affair—
with enough choices in the front yard
for a blossomy puff worthy of Fragonard,
instead expends its single breath
beneath one leathery leaf of loquat
which flops over and again lies flat.
Spring is frivolous like that.

A Plain Ordinary Steel Needle Can Float on Pure Water

—Ripley's *Believe It or Not!*

Who hasn't seen
a plain ordinary
steel needle float serene
on water as if lying on a pillow?
The water cuddles up like Jell-O.
It's a treat to see water
so rubbery, a needle
so peaceful, the point encased
in the tenderest dimple.
It seems so *simple*
when things or people
have modified each other's qualities
somewhat;
we almost forget the oddity
of that.

Distance

The texts
are insistent:
it takes two points
to make a distance.

The cubit,
for instance,
is nothing
till you use it.

Then it is rigid
and bracelike;
it has actual strength.

Something metal
runs through
every length—

.

the very armature
of love, perhaps.

Only distance
lets distance collapse.

The Vessel and the Cup

from a Hasidic story

What cup knows the distress
of the large vessel, knows
any more than two inches
of the purple? For the cup,
everything that fills it up
is equal—the little jug,
the pot, the large vessel.
Beyond its own meniscus
nothing's knowable for a cup.
But the vessel wishes
one something
could use it up.

Wooden

In the presence of supple
goodness, some people
grow less flexible,
experiencing a woodenness
they wouldn't have thought possible.
It is as strange and paradoxical
as the combined suffering
of Pinocchio and Geppetto
if Pinocchio had turned and said,
I can't be human after all.

The Second

In any collision, one strikes;
the other is stricken. This
is a given with the nano-
calculations made possible
through silicon.
Earlier centuries depended
on testimony to know
the bender from the bent,
and often judged an act
by how it ended. Many bumps
were simply abandoned to the
morass of simultaneous action.
Love being among them.
For who would be second
as I find myself second—
the original feathered weapon
tattered, *I love you* seconded
for seven years. Whose love

comes second forever bears
a quiver of unsayable words,
unusable gestures; a boldness
lost—as if Ruth had not said,
Whither thou goest, but merely gone,
making Naomi's people her people,
her home her home.

Heat

There is a heat
coming off
anything we meet
our-sized and
mildly round.
Who has not found
herself warmed
by certain stones,
for example, or
made occasional
"mistakes" about things
that didn't turn out
to be people?
Perhaps we
share a shape
that loves itself,

a heat anterior
to life, further back
than hearts.
I postulate
a very early date
for when the warming
starts.

Poetry in Translation

It is
so snug—
the skin
of the living animal
stretched out
to a rug
shaped something
like the United States.
One meditates
upon a
Florida-like flap—
a forward leg
which ran
the Russian steppes
perhaps?

If She Only Had One Minute

What would she put in it?
She wouldn't *put*
she thinks; she would *take*,
suck it up
like a deep lake—
bloat indiscriminate
on her last instant—
feast on everything she
had released, dismissed, or
pushed away; she would make
room and room as though
her whole life of resistance
had been for this one purpose:
on the last minute of the last day
she would drink and have it; ballooning
like a gravid salmon or the moon.

Elephant Rocks

Here and there,
at the edges and marges,
a bit of an elephant surfaces—
a dome and a dip, a haunch
or an aspect of head—
some worn-away soft and yet
angular hump of the
shambling elephant armature,
up through the earth—a bump
or a knob with the elephant signature.
The ancient, implacable creature
comes ambling back; a bulge
reemerges, that sober, that
giveaway gray. The dirt
rubs away from a treasure
too patient and deep to be lost,
however we've hurt, whatever
we've done to the beasts,
whatever we say.